Destination Cuba
A Cuba Memoir

Richard M. Grove

Hidden Brook Press

First Edition

Hidden Brook Press
www.HiddenBrookPress.com
writers@HiddenBrookPress.com

Copyright © 2014 Hidden Brook Press
Copyright © 2014 Richard M. Grove

All rights for writing revert to the author. All rights for book, layout and design remain with Hidden Brook Press. No part of this book may be reproduced except by a reviewer who may quote brief passages in a review. The use of any part of this publication reproduced, transmitted in any form or by any means, electronic, mechanical, photocopied, recorded or otherwise stored in a retrieval system without prior written consent of the publisher is an infringement of the copyright law.

Destination Cuba: A Cuba Memoir
by Richard M. Grove

Layout and Design – Richard M. Grove
Cover Design – Richard M. Grove
Cover Photograph – Richard M. Grove
B/W Photographs – Richard M. Grove

Printed and bound in Canada

Typeset in Garamond

Library and Archives Canada Cataloguing in Publication

Grove, Richard M. (Richard Marvin), 1953-, author
 Destination Cuba : a Cuba memoir / Richard M. Grove.

ISBN 978-1-927725-10-8 (pbk.)

 1. Grove, Richard M. (Richard Marvin), 1953- -- Travel--Cuba. 2. Cuba--Description and travel. 3. Cuba--Poetry. I. Title.

PS8563.R75D47 2014   C818'.609   C2014-903567-5

Jorge

Wency

This book is dedicated to
my dear Cuban brothers:
Manuel, Jorge and little brother Wency,
and their generously welcoming families.

Thank you
all for showing me your Cuba

and to my darling travelling wife, Kim.

Manuel

Destination Cuba
A Cuba Memoir

Memoir Chapters:
– Another Arrival in Cuba – *p. 1*
– All Is Well That Ends Well – *p. 15*
– A Pilgrimage to the José Martí Monument – *p. 55*

Poems:
– In a Wave of Black They Shattered – *p. 6*
– Donkey Cart – *p. 7*
– The Sucking Waves – *p. 8*
– Cuban Winter Rain – *p. 9*
– What is this Obsession with Cuban Laundry – *p. 10*
– The Pride of Cuba – *p. 11*
– Cuban Flowers – *p. 12*
– Blue Breeze Whips – *p. 13*
– Without a Word – *p. 48*
– Listening With Cuban Ears – *p. 49*
– January 28, 2014 Arrival – *p. 50*
– Holguín, Cuba 2003 Vignette – # 1 – *p. 84*
– Holguín, Cuba 2003 Vignette – # 2 – *p. 85*
– Holguín, Cuba 2003 Vignette – # 3 – *p. 86*
– Holguín, Cuba 2003 Vignette – # 4 – *p. 87*
– Holguín, Cuba 2003 Vignette – # 5 – *p. 88*
– Holguín, Cuba 2003 Vignette – # 6 – *p. 89*
– From Holguín to Gibara and Back Again – *p. 92*
– The Round – *p. 94*

– Author Bio - *p. 96*

Another Arrival in Cuba

I disembarked from the exceedingly cramped flying sardine can that SunWing calls an airplane to the heavy breezeless air of Holguín's steaming tarmac. It was 7:30pm when I sauntered down the tall silver stairs. The low hanging brilliant full moon lit the stoically standing silent palms that lined the runway. 28oc drooped motionless. In the future we have to remember to fly with WestJet. There is always enough room for my knees and they never chisel you out of taking an extra shirt or jar of peanut butter because your bag is a snitch over weight. In fact they have me registered as the president of the Canada Cuba Literary Alliance (CCLA) and have always given Kim and me free full bags of luggage for humanitarian reasons when we are taking computers, books and clothes to Cuba.

To my surprise and delight I was the third person in line waiting to go through customs. I was hyped and ready to get a cab. One person went through customs and I moved up a few inches in line to the restlessly eager second position, one person from freedom. I stood motionless with my eyes gently closed waiting my turn. Low and behold when I opened my eyes only a moment later there were ten family members joining the person in line ahead of me – ten. Two of them were whining tired children clawing at mother's legs. Patience Tai, patience. I stood there like a pillar of salt, lips zipped. As it turned out they were all from China with red passports – I did not hear a single word of English among them. They progressed through the line painstakingly slowly. I looked behind me to see that the previously long line was slowly evaporating. Eventually I was the first and the last in my line. It became obvious that I should have abandoned my stoic patience long ago and joined others in faster queues. By the time I was through customs, with hardly a single question, I was then faced with two long lines going through the x-ray machines. I quickly abandoned the whirling line of rowdy twenty-year-olds gyrating with the pulsing hoots of "we want beer, we want beer!!!!" By the time I was through the line I was the third last. From being third to first in line to third to last took about an hour but there in the distance was a cart with my bicycle and luggage already stacked. How and why I do not know but I was grateful that there were angels looking out for me, stacking my luggage.

I stepped through the parting, sliding doors to glowing yellow lights. The first cab driver that approached me had a small white 1962 Russian Lada. I rejected his in-your-face offer of a ride simply because he had no roof rack for my boxed bicycle. The next car in line was a 1958 Studebaker with an ample roof rack, the size of a Cuban child's bedroom. A sixtyish greying Cuban man, with similar ample girth as mine, stood silently unimpressed by my volume of luggage. *Taxi señor?* was uttered with a slight welcoming smile and nod. He was not about to get too excited about the prospect of a Canadian tourist in the need of a taxi. His nonchalant demeanor impressed me. I wheeled my brimming cart towards him, *Si señor*. I ran my hand over the brush painted yellow bumper of his enduring monument to Cuban ingenuity. The ripples of imperfection reminded me of a thousand Cuban cars I have seen lovingly maintained with the budget of a working stiff.

I have been coming to Cuba for so many years that I have forgotten the necessity of proper arrival preparation. My lackadaisical departure from Toronto did not have me print out the full address of my destination, *mi amigo* Manuel. Broken English and broken Spanish led me to drawing a crude map of where I was going. With the assistance of about ten other cab drivers, all hovering in the light of the Studebaker's high beams, we nattered at each other gesticulating in the general direction of my destination. My pen was passed back and forth as others added geographic features to my crinkled napkin until everyone agreed on not only the destination but also the exact street short cuts that would have me arrive in good time.

There was no air conditioning, mug racks, fancy LED lit dashboard or purring stereo but there was by god a pivoting-triangle window that unlocked with a snap. It swiveled open pouring the sweet aroma of fresh cut hay into the face of this tired traveler.

Once again I awoke to the neighbour's rooster crowing, the other neighbour's pigs snorting and yet another neighbour's dog barking. As my eyes quivered open to the 6:30am golden stream of morning I realized without a question that I was in Cuba. The only thing missing was my darling Kim. My pot of *té fria,* cold tea was already sitting in the fridge waiting for me – made the night before. All I needed was my cup of granola and I was set for the morning. By 7:30am I was back curled up with my skimpy Cuban pillow. I stirred for the second time about 10:30am. By 11am I was tapping on my computer, by noon I was stretching, bare bellied, in the now high-in-the-sky sun followed by a face up basking in glory.

In a Wave of Black
They Shattered

Twenty-five or maybe thirty *toti*
with unceremonious clatter
fluttered their way into the large tree
that sheltered the back yard
of our *casa*.
Like children descending
on a quiet school yard
they joyously invaded
our quiet breakfast
and then in a wave
of black they shattered
the brilliant blue sky
and departed.

Donkey Cart

It's always busy and buzzing here in Holguín
the pig next door roots, snorts and squeals
in red earth of forever hard
at the same time as chickens cluck and scratch
for invisible specks untossed
while the rooster struts and crows his superiority
over time and rising sun while the dog yelps and
the children cry with delight.

The streets buzz past the silent workers carried
by the clatter of donkey carts while trucks
zip in and out belching at zinging motorcycles.
That is just how it is here.
That is just how it looks and sounds
every day, day after day, forever buzzing,
never stopping until
night turns on the music and the island sings.

That is just how it is here.
All of a sudden trucks have nothing to do.
Children and motorcycles have been put to rest.
Souls are let to dance
but the donkey cart clatter continues
late into the night.

The Sucking Waves

The sea was filled
with rage last night.
Foaming, churning,
whipped to crashing crests.
Low led clouds
shed shafts of cold rain
careening to dancing beach
pitted deep.

Flung beyond surf line
blue swollen man-of-war
laying in wait for foaming
burst to carry them back
on sucking waves.

Today calmed to placid blue
under dour pink.
Sacrificial lambs strewn
lifeless
poisonous purple tentacles dead
yet still poised
for unsuspecting
tourist victim's tread.

Cuban Winter Rain

Last night there was
a very gentle sparse rain
on our very dry meadows.
Today it is sunny and hot,
the aroma of dry grass
once again fills the air.
Whims of the tropics
in winter.

Manuel Leon and Richard Grove collaboration

What is this Obsession with Cuban Laundry?

I have photographs of colourful towels
hanging from laundry lines
strung between weather beaten window frame
and slanted rusty pole.

I have photographs of skimpy, pretty, pink panties
hanging unabashedly, side by side
with warn, ugly, grey, underpants,
gigantic boxers.

I have an artistic, carefully composed,
photographic study of white sheets fluttering
against dazzling blue, Cuban skies.
Stunning brilliance, beating.

I have pictures of socks hanging, heels worn,
toes pushed through, dripping. No yarn to darn,
pointing down to grassless
red earth of smooth swept backyard.

I have snapshots of sexy lace brasiers,
Che t-shirts, pants, all scrubbed clean,
hanging in noonday Cuban heat
winging freely after a hard day of labour.

What is this obsession with Cuban laundry.
Is it art or social commentary,
statements about clean hearts and a loving people
or just laundry!

The Pride of Cuba

Strung from rusted
TV antenna to eves
the pride of Cuba, clean
waves from roof tops.

White sheets greet
brisk Cuban breeze,
flapping a salute to blue.

Cuban Flowers

Purple flowered drapes hang
poised in front of blue wall
dripping, drenched in sun
stunning, stripped with green.
No political interpretation needed
just clean drapes drying.

Bright flower sheets hang
over rusty iron railing
flapping,
dripping the smell of clean
onto hot pavement, below
No political interpretation needed
just flower sheets hanging.

Gold school uniform, proudly
flails in stiff
sun-soaked gusts
waiting the youth of today
the flowers of Cuba,
to dawn with pride.
No political interpretation needed
just uniform flapping.

Blue Breeze Whips

Pink pajamas attack
yellow towel
flailing
white bikini underpants
sexy
caressed by sleeve of white shirt
brown pants drip
puddle
pools in dust
little bird dips
blue breeze whips
the pride of tomorrow.

All Is Well That Ends Well

One year our dear friend Wency – I call him – *mi hermano pequeño* – my little brother, took us to the small seaside town of La Herradura, looking for a *casa particular* – bed and breakfast. Our goal that year was to have a non-resort beach holiday. It is not that we have anything against the typical beach-resort holiday, we have loved being the pampered, lazy, over-fed tourist, many times in the past, but to use a common phrase "been there, done that". For that year we were looking for a more Cuban flavoured holiday away from the tourist hubbub. We wanted to stay "with the people" as it were, though how can a tourist paying a fee to a Cuban family for the "best" bed in the house ever really be considered "with the people?"

In previous years we have spent plenty of

time in *casa particulars* but most always at, diesel-truck-fume-spewing, inner-city locations. The La Herradura year we wanted soft sand and surf. With Wency's help we loaded our bicycles on to the rusted roof-rack of a 1958 Russian Volga taxi. It was a classic Russian gem, brush painted by hand with Cuban-flag-blue house paint. It rattled like an old lady dragging a bucket of bolts. It lurched from a stand still reminding us that there were no seatbelts. This was not your typical Cuban airport taxi.

Heading to La Herradura

Luggage and bikes stowed we headed to La Herradura weaving through lush emerald valleys snaked by narrow winding rivers. The scenery on the way was stunningly gorgeous. The sky was Cuban blue shining over swaying palms. From Holguín we travelled North West past tiny towns, first Uñas and then Velasco. We brushed the shores of the shimmering lake Presa Cacoyoguin — no speed boats or jet skis on these calm, unspoiled, waters. Within an hour and a half we arrived searching for our prearranged *casa*.

This quiet little town was in sleep mode. It is a Cuban national's summer destination for fun on the beach but not a winter tourist destination for non-Cubans — the place was dead. A few chickens clucked from shade to shade, a black and white goat nudged gently through the spiny grass. With nimble lips and dexterous tongue she cropped the vegetation close to the ground. She seemed not to care that we were the only tourists to be seen.

Driving up and down a few pot-holed roads, dodging a rather amiable black pig we found our way to Maria's front door, a stone's throw from a slightly unkempt beach. The house was clean and polished, a government inspected *casa particulars* standard that we were used to. Maria was a genial, stooped, elderly lady who welcomed us with open arms. *Entra, entra en* – Come in, come in – she greeted us, motioning that we should follow her to our room. We meandered through the long narrow house dragging out bags to the back door. It swung open with her gentle nudge.

In the Front Door
and Out the Back

Well where the heck was our room? We walked in the front door, through the house and out the back door. We crept past piles of brick and cement rubble, ducked under a line laden with clean laundry wafting gently in the late morning breeze; we passed by a dilapidated brick wall that looked like it might have once been part of the house. We wove through a thorn infested back yard to a dusty narrow lane lined by weather beaten wooden shacks. Maria pressed a key into the door that was to be our home away from home. With a smile she waved, *hasta la vista.*

    We groped our way into the cool darkness of a well-worn 1960s kitchen, setting our bags down on dusty furniture, a table that wobbled, a chair that creaked. Oh… my… God!! What have we gotten ourselves into? With hesitation we made our way through to the bedroom, beyond that the bathroom, a spider's web tickled across my face. The bedroom was a dark windowless room with one bare light bulb that swung from the centre of the greying ceiling. The bathroom was formerly tiled from floor to ceiling. Over the last 40 or 50 years tiles had been replaced, fallen out and replaced many times. The mosaic patchwork of time was, at the least, an interesting montage of poverty, indifference and distain. Was the crowning glory of our tour the rat that scurried through the hole in the bathroom wall or the cockroaches that scuttled down the drain? I will repeat – Oh... my... God!! What have we gotten ourselves into?

Well maybe some fresh air and a walk on the beach would bring some reasonable perspective to the situation. This room was not up to the standard of our previous *casa particular* stays. I started to wonder if these rooms were ever inspected by the government. I visualized the blind inspector tapping his way through the room with silver coins, a bribe, pressed in his hot little hand. Well we did want a more Cuban experience; surely this was not it. By the time we had a long walk on the beach, a swim and a beach side hotdog we were ready for a long sleep. After a careful inspection of the bed and pillows we hesitantly, cautiously, hunkered down for the night.

A Good Night's Sleep

The bed was moderately comfortable and I have to admit that we slept well in the deserted quietude of this virtual ghost town. In the morning we were greeted by a blinding sun that felt more like midday than early morning. There is no getting away from waking up with either a crowing rooster or the blaring sun when you are in Cuba. The first thing on the agenda was a walk on the beach and see what breakfast items the sleepy-town-beach-side, kiosk might have. The walk was wonderful; the dip in the calm ocean was like dipping one's soul into fresh orange juice after a walk in the desert. The name of the kiosk was *Todo para el día* – All for the Day, or something like that. It definitely was not "All for the Morning" – it was closed but the good news was that it would open soon.

Hotdog With or Without a Bun

A quarter mile walk on the deserted beach around the small bay and back had us arrive at an open sign – the front plywood door was now flipped up shading the counter. We approached to see what they might have for breakfast. We were delighted by the long and detailed menu but the availability was short and precise. Hotdog with or without a bun or an omelet. I said to Wency – "I will have one of each but isn't a hotdog without a bun just a wiener?" We laughed out loud and smacked the counter with a hilarious echoing thud that rippled across the deserted beach.

We have been to Cuba many, many times. We have learned that a menu is not a list of what food they can serve you but rather it is a list of what they would like to serve you. My ongoing joke when we walk into a restaurant is "would you like pork or chicken or would you like chicken or pork." No matter what is on the menu you will have one or the other. At this kiosk the question is "would you like a hotdog with a bun or would you like a hotdog without a bun?"

Wency encouraged us to sit a little ways away in the shade and he would bring us our omelet and hotdogs. He finally approached us with a big grin on his face and his hands behind his back. "I have some good news and I have some bad news my friends. The good news is that I have a hotdog for each of you but the bad news is that it is not cooked." He pulled his hands from behind him and presented a cold pink wiener stuck in a tiny tea biscuit size bun. So picture this, two inches of the uncooked pink wiener conspicuously protruded from each side of a little white hump. All we could do was laugh. I called it a little white cushion with a wiener. No mustard, no ketchup and no relish. I still laugh every time I think of it. The menu should have said, would you like a cold uncooked wiener on a tiny bun or would you like an uncooked wiener. Laugh, laugh, laugh.

The omelet was a dog of a different name. It was just as funny looking but maybe more pathetic. One greasy deep-fried egg arrived, splayed on the same kind of small fat white bun.

Oh the other part of the breakfast menu

is that they did not have *agua con gas* – water with gas, as the sign said they had, so I ordered a coke that they did not have so I ordered a *lemon con gas* – lemon pop with gas, that they did not have so we all three had orange pop. The orange pop was a perfect complementary beverage to go with an uncooked wiener on a tiny bun. Laugh, laugh, laugh. To put as positive of a spin on the breakfast as possible I have to say that the orange pop was *magnifico*.

Time to Move On

Ok so just how many days did we want to share our room with a rat and cockroaches and have uncooked wieners and orange pop for breakfast. I think the choice was clear. It was time to move on.

We returned to our room and sat in the shade of our sand filled front porch talking about our options. It is obvious that this is not the Canadian dream holiday on the beach so what are our alternatives. We had already discovered that there was not a single car in La Herradura to take us to the next town even if we were willing to take our chances that there would be a room. The only option was for Wency and me to bicycle to La Boca, the next town 15km away and see what was available. We only had two bicycles so Kim would stay with the luggage while Wency and I headed out in the now blistering heat of noon. The good thing is that the road was moderately flat and straight – we made good speed. The flora and fauna were sparse and low. On our right was the ever steady ocean sparkling in its never ending undulations. On the left were ocean sault encrusted tidal pools that stretched for miles. Terns and Flamingos dotted the quiet mud flats undisturbed by our gentle passing.

Arriving at La Boca

We had the pleasure of staying in La Boca for a full week. Every morning was greeted with a swim in the ocean. Jacketed, Cuban workers congregated at the dock waiting for their, sometimes-daily-ferry ride across the channel to their truck transport to Puerto Padre, where they would work, visit or shop. The common statement that was uttered as they saw us swimming was – *?Es muy fría mi amigo?* – It is very cold my friend? We swam morning noon and night all week. The beach, the ocean, the sun and even the roaming pigs could not have been more enchanting. When the cab arrived on our last day we were sad to leave. It was such a calm and refreshing holiday.

The literal translation of La Boca is The Mouth. The town of La Boca is situated on the east side of the mouth of a bay with the town of Socucho on the west side. A small standing room only ferry transports people and sundry back and forth a dozen times a day. Most of the people being ferried to Socucho are coming to or from Puerto Padre. The town of La Boca is literally at the end of the road. *Carretera 21-* Road 21 ends at Playa La Boca – La Boca beach. If you go any further you end up in the channel, the shipping lane that takes ocean going cargo ships, south into the bustling, handsome city of Peurto Padre. The shipping channel is so long and narrow it looks like a wide river. It is in fact the entrance to a huge secluded salt-water bay.

The small, end-of-the-road town, La Boca, turned out to be a wonderfully-magical place. The aura was totally different from La Herradura. It was as closed down as La Herradura but not as dead. Things were instantly recognizably different. First of all there were more locals out-and-about smiling and waving to us as we passed by. The roaming pigs and chickens were the same, the sky, the sun, the beach, the swaying palms, were all the same but somehow there was a different sense of life in this little town. There were no tourists. All of the *casa particulars* were empty – some were closed for the season.

We had no problem finding a room,

almost right on the beach. A small blue swinging gate, at the front of the house, was never locked. When we arrived we were welcomed by a smiling, round-faced Cuban woman, the owner of the house. She instantly made us welcome. Our room led out onto the family patio area where people came and went ducking under daily laundry that fluttered in the La Boca breeze. Around the corner of the house was a vine shaded area with a table where I worked on my laptop most mornings.

The one thing that was the same was the fact that there was no car in the town. Everywhere Wency and I looked and asked we were greeted with the same answer – tomorrow maybe Jorge will come with his car. *Mañana, mañana*. Tomorrow, tomorrow there will be a car coming, I hope, I think, maybe. Wency and I searched the town high and low looking for a car that might take us back to La Herradura to pick up Kim and the luggage. Finally we found a Cuban tourist and low and behold Wency knew the girlfriend of the friend of the owner. They were packing up to leave their rented house and would be going past La Herradura but there was no room in the car for everyone to go in one trip. The long and the short of it is that many hours later we had Kim and the luggage, two bikes, Wency and me all in one place at our new *casa particular*. It was a long adventurous day of being delivered out of the bondage of what will always be known as *La casa con la rata y cucarachas* – The casa with the rat and cockroaches.

We celebrated our first cooling evening with a fine dinner at a restaurant at the back of a house. They were not legally allowed to serve tourists meals but as is most often the case, when there is an opportunity to earn a few dollars rules are bent. $4 = 4CUC (each) bought us a fine shrimp dinner with plenty of left overs to go to our *casa* for lunch tomorrow. It was a long adventurous day. All is well that ends well – Todo está bien que termina bien.

A Week in La Boca

Wency is such a good little brother. He stayed with us for a few nights but eventually he had to head back to *Holguín* to family and work. The three of us took the little ferry across the channel to Socucho. The ferry is simply a 15 foot dory with an inboard motor and a small house for a steering wheel. Once everyone was aboard with boxes and bags of all description it seemed to me that there was no room for the three of us let alone our two bikes but sure enough in perfect Cuban style the bikes were gently handed down and perched on the steering housing. They stood politely with a stranger holding them erect; no room to lay them down. The tiny boat bobbed back and forth gently with every movement we made, it is a good job the sea was calm. In a morbid flash of fear I envisioned me diving to the bottom of the channel looking for my somewhat-expensive camera that swayed gently around my neck.

On the Socucho side we disembarked with the same nimble stride, offering a hand and receiving a hand of support as we leapt to the solid wharf. Bikes were passed with lively ease from the strong arms of a friendly Cuban passenger. The sense of friendly camaraderie was warming. On solid ground we stood in the shade of the Socucho Hotel waiting for our transport truck that would take 40 or 50 of us 12km to Puerto Padre where Kim and I would say goodbye to Wency.

One day I had a little Cuban boy hovering over me while I typed. He was thrilled to see a computer and the letters magically appearing. With his help I made some asterisks into the shape of a face. I had him type the asterisks while I operated the return and space buttons. He laughed and thought that it was pretty cool. He called his grandmother and patted himself on the chest while he jabbered, in Spanish, about his accomplishment. We might have a future digital designer on our hands.

```
          ******
        ************
      ******************
    *                      *
   **      ***      ***        **
  *          *        *           *
  *                  **           *
  **                             **
        *       *****      *
         *                *
            ***       ***
             *         *
      ********      ********
     *********      *********
    **********      **********
             *        *
             *        *
             *        *
              *    *
                *
```

Hold the Chicken,
Hold the Mayo,
Hold the Butter,
Hold the Lettuce

On our first La Boca morning we had eggs, wieners and bread for breakfast with orange pop and espresso coffee. Wency and I were out for an early morning walk on the beach and bought six eggs for 1.5 Cubano pesos each = about $0.06 each egg (less than half the price of eggs at Canadian prices), plus some bread for a total of 1 CUC. They were purchased from a lunch cafeteria kiosk at the end of the beach.

We are in such a small seaside village that there are no real stores. There are three or four kiosks mostly selling pop, beer and a few convenience items. We bought the buns and eggs not because they sold buns and eggs but because they sold them to us as if we bought one of their menu items. It reminds me of the Jack Nicolson movie "Five Easy Pieces" where he orders plain toast. "We don't sell plain toast" "Then I will have a toasted chicken salad sandwich, hold the chicken, hold the mayo, hold the butter, hold the lettuce." The wieners were purchased from a hotdog vender.

Prospects in La Boca

We are literally at the end of the road. For us it is the end of a car ride but for many Cubans it is the end of the road in a metaphoric way. 15km down the coastal road, where we came from, is the town of La Herradura where there are no opportunities. In this town of La Boca where we are staying at Philipa and Blanca's *casa particular*, one would have the same limited options. In the summer months, each town becomes a bustle of Cuban beach visitors. There would be some temporary income during those two months. For more than those two months one would have to leave town, be a fisherman or work in one of the infrequently visited kiosks.

The one thing that they have going for themselves in La Boca is the quiet and solitude, though I don't know how marketable quiet and solitude are in Cuba. It reminds me of how quiet our house in Presqu'ile Provincial Park is. For our B&B, quiet is a marketable commodity. For Kim and me the quiet is a wonderful attribute. In La Boca, during the middle of the week there are no Cubans on the beach and little to no activity, though it apparently gets busy with Cubans in the hot summer, using the place as a seaside bathing destination. The expanding hotel just three *casas* down the street is proof that something must happen in this lazy town at some point. Maybe that is when the *Pizza Calienta* – Hot Pizza, kiosk that is on the beach will open. I wish it were open now. The deserted quality of these two seaside villages, in some ways, reminds me of Wasaga Beach or Port Dover. Hustle bustle in the summer and utterly deserted in the winter.

The Truck Ride to Puerto Padre

Kim and I became excited tourists willing to squeeze onto a local Cubano transport truck, with our bicycles and head to Puerto Padre simply for the adventure. We left on a Sunday morning in order to accompany our dear friend Wency who was going specifically to find a ride back to *Holguín*. We rose at 5:30am to roosters crowing in the dark. Not even the dogs or roaming pigs were awake. Kim made instant decaf coffee, strong, to mimic Cuban espresso. It was a moderately good substitute for the real thing.

We were on the dock waiting for the first ferry by 6:20am. Cubans started to gather shortly after us for the first transport of the day. The three of us and two bicycles were, in our humble estimation, about half the load capacity for the small boat. By the time we left seven more passengers and a small crate of chickens joined us for our standing room only, bobbing, journey.

On the other side we joined the growing, milling, gaggle of Cubans waiting for the public transport truck that travelled back and forth between Socucho and Las Tunas. Our truck was a 40 or 50 year old flat-bed with canvas walls and roof. Under cover, out of the tormenting sun, there were four board benches that held 10 or 11 people shoulder to shoulder on each bench and 10 or more standing in the two middle isles holding a bar attached to the steel roof. This truck, on a squeeze, would hold 60 – 70 people. It had a ladder on the back end that would take passengers up into the large metal box.

Forty-three of us packed into this rumbling metal death trap. No one kissed the ground when we arrived in Puerto Padre. This is a pretty normal type of transportation taking passengers from city to city. The bicycles were passed in after we settled onto our hard seats. The bikes were stood in the aisles held erect up by fellow travellers. A box of live young turkeys chattered at one end of the bikes while at the other end a mother nursed her new born. Everyone was literally shoulder to shoulder. Sweat ran from my brow and dripped from my bearded chin.

The ride was amazing in many ways. For that 45 minutes we were, so called, with the people. I have travelled many hours on such trucks and the experience is always the same. The air might be dusty, the noise of the tires spinning over pavement or gravel is loud and intrusive but the love, the sense of camaraderie is palpable. Not just because we were intimately connected to the lady singing to her cradled baby but because we were all physically, intimately connected shoulder to shoulder moving as one, swaying, tipping, jerking as one interconnected consciousness. When someone landed in your lap you simply smiled and said *mucho gusto* – nice to meet you. When someone's turkey or chicken nibbles at your leg you smiled with others, all knowing that the little feathered critter will soon be someone's dinner

There was a long, uncanvassed, window on each side of the truck that allowed needed air to flow. The down side to this is that the dust from the dirt road wafted in every time we stopped. The nursing baby was covered by a clean white blanket to protect it from the red molecular landscape that filtered down over us all.

We travelled at a comfortable speed weaving around the occasional large pothole and driving down onto the well-travelled shoulder of the road from time to time. It was an interesting opportunity to watch the people as they jostled back and forth. There was no sense of private or personal space. My leg was wedged between the persons legs that faced me. My shoulders were constantly pressed to or bumping each of the travelers beside me. There was no room for ego on that truck. Two men joked and had fun with each other. When one faded and fell asleep with bobbing head his friend pulled him close and put his friend's head on his shoulder; such loving generosity. A woman held her hand out to me to pull her forward into a vacant sitting spot. Another leaned on me heavily as she pressed to the back of the truck to get out. We were all in this together. Everyone smiled and nodded back and forth.

A Meander
Around Puerto Padre

Puerto Padre is a delightful precious little city with a sense of hustle bustle about it. A bright sun glinted off the church steeple, through swaying palms to the well-kept streets. After a short meander we took the hesitant steps into a street side pavilion that sold hotdogs. I announced to Wency that I would like mine uncooked please. Low and behold the hotdog was not only cooked but there was mustard, relish and even a napkin. A 12 inch fried wiener peeped out from each end of an 8 inch bun. The CNE could not have made a better hotdog.

After a calming stroll by the stone walled waterfront that looked north towards La Boca we said goodbye to Wency. Kim and I mounted our steel steeds and headed back the 12km to Socucho. By now the day had grown hot in the full sun of the late morning but we were not in any hurry. A sip of water and we were off.

18km
In the Morning Heat

Sticking to the shady side of the road as much as possible we headed north towards the ocean. City scape soon turned to suburban yarded houses, turned to pastures and farm yards and finally wide open vistas. Then with the curve in the road the landscape turned to bleak red mud flats with a raised road that crawled across the barren desolation of cracked earth. Crystalized salt structures grew in sun-shrinking, lifeless pools. The day baked on. It was not long before we yearned for shade. The road was lined by stunted shrubs that stood no taller than chest high. The afternoon sun began to roast our enthusiasm.

The road grew very flat, *muy plana* and was moderately well maintained, though unpaved. This road was the only link between Socucho and Puerto Padre. There is nothing, absolutely nothing, but salt mud flats and scrubland. No tree grew higher than eight feet. As we biked our way in the heat we longed for a single tree that might cast a shadow more than waist high, that we could stand in while we had a drink and a gaze at the wonderment of this flat baron land.

A Pink Ribbon

Half way on our journey, out of the corner of my eye, I saw a cackling pink stripe in one of the distant shallow bays. We turned around and passed through the brush at a spot in the road that looked like it used to be a turnaround area during construction. We bicycled a half mile over the cracked mud flats dodging some rough patches of an ancient coral bed. We laid our bikes down and walked to the muddy, shallow shore where a few species of shore birds tiptoed the lightly lapping shore. A quarter mile beyond that were two or three hundred gorgeous pink flamingos schooled in a long narrow crimson line. It was amazing to see and hear them. Few would have ever noticed them as they plodded past to or from Socucho. It was definitely the thrill of the day.

I quickly took off my shoes and socks, grabbed my video camera and ventured out into the still water. Warm silken mud squished between my toes as I inched toward the gaggling ribbon of pink. Red sucking mud slowed every step. Kim, standing on shore, gradually shrank in the distance. Her worries grew the further I got to hollering distance.

My pressing goal was to see them fly but they were not to be stirred. In desperation I flapped my arms, swung my shirt over my head and yelled threatening hooping calls in hopes that I might stir them into flight. At first, the lazy colony took little notice of me as I carefully squished through the murky, knee-deep water. Not even a lifting of their heads in wonder were they bothered by my presence. The more I flapped and hollered the more I slowly sunk into the thick cloying mud. The further I went the more difficult it grew to walk. Wisdom soon dictated that I should venture no further despite still being too far away to get a reasonable quality picture for posterity. With disappointment I finally turned to suck my way back towards the shore's edge.

With flapping gesticulations Kim pointed for me to turn around. With no provocation, silence erupted into a cacophony of worry. Their cackles grew more perturbed until they finally leapt from their safe vantage point and slapped their way into the stunning blue sky. In an explosion, the panoramic vista was filled with a chaos of pink. Squawks of displeasure packed the brilliant blue sky with pink flapping, then, within moments, all was quiet. I stood dumbfounded by the wave upon wave of pink swirls. I was awestruck by the pink ribbon of ecstasy that now quilted the blue sky in rolling undulations.

Upon arriving back at the crackled red shore Kim confessed her nervousness. "That log in the distance looked like it was a sleeping alligator. I was watching to see if it was going to wake up before I yelled for you to come back." Cuba does have alligators though only in the northern *Zapata* Swamps but Kim did not know that. I am quite certain that I could not have outrun a slithering alligator and I never want to test the issue.

Feet dried and shoed we were finally back on our bikes heading to Socucho. By now the temperature must have been between 35 and 40oc and still not a speck of shade to be seen. Every peddle push was an arduous test of our endurance. Our water was low and we were getting hungry. I announced to Kim that we were about half way now. This cruel joke was discouraging for her. Thank heavens five minutes later we were at the ferry dock cooling in the shade of the Socucho *Hotel* waiting for the approaching ferry. What a stupendous day.

The Lighthouse Climb

With energy left, we headed west along the shore in search of the lighthouse that we had previously only had a glimpse of through the trees. Four kilometers along a rough road took us to a small, delicate lighthouse perched on an eight-foot high concrete platform. This was no tourist destination with convenient handrails and safety bars. The precarious climb to the foot of the lighthouse made me wonder if I should continue. The narrow, vertical ladder attached to the hollow echoing interior led me, hand over hand, to a dramatic view that was worth the heart-thumping climb. I took a few white-knuckle seconds of video before cautiously, ever so slowly, returning to the ground. The climb would have better been done at a more nimble time in my life.

Putting our feet up at our La Boca *casa* was as delightful as if we had landed at a five star resort.

Without a Word

When you came to me
it was just a little past noon
and still the rooster rose
above a distant clarinet
scaling up then down
        up then down
in practiced perfection.

I had intended
to sit in the Cuban sun
and read the wisdom of José Martí,
ponder his words and meditate
but the longing call
of my rooster friend
drew me to the top
of the stuccoed wall.
There in the shimmering green
of a Bioba tree
I was instantly,
without a word
with you and Martí.

Listening With Cuban Ears

Dedicated to Colin Morton

I lay reading on my bed by the open window
of my second-story room at Hotel Atlantico in Cuba
on an early February night when I heard
a swell from the ocean a short distance away.

It rose and echoed through the sleeping corridors
like the distant thunder of a stadium
where the ghost of José Martí
now speaks to the masses.

The rhythm of hush and roar, hush and roar
is suspended between sleep and waking
between listening and reading.

Book now on chest rising and falling
between hush and roar.
One moment I am in the stadium listening
with Cuban ears, the next I am
in my bed, traveller, listening to the rushing sea.

This poem was written Feb, 2009 at the end of the CCLA trip to Holguin, Cuba where Colin gave me his book. Portions of the first lines of this poem are from, and based on, Colin Morton's poem "Prologue, with Anecdote of the I's" from his book "Dance, Misery" isbn - 0-9689723-8-1 published by Seraphim Editions — a fine book of poetry.

January 28, 2014 Arrival

(On the birthday of José Julián Martí Pérez)

Dear Lionel:

I am thinking about you
while sitting under a Cuban palm
wafted by a warm January ocean breeze
with the ghost of Jose Marti lapping
at my pale Canadian ankles.

We received the news
of your January 25th planetary arrival
from the womb to cradling arms.
You may have already met Marti
before you arrived. His 161st birthday
was today, three days after yours.
I have only met the freedom
that he fought and died for.

Your mother emailed our dear
Cuban sister Adonay the news.
Adonay told my brother Manuel,
Manuel told little brother Wency
then finally Wency phoned Kim and me
at the Club Amigo Hotel in Guardalavaca.
All of your Cuban family is delighted
by your safe arrival
but no one more than I.

We have all shared kisses and hugs
besos y abrazos
and can only imagine your pink puckered toes,
your wrinkled worry-free brow,
ten tiny fisted fingers
eager to explore your new reality
of sights unseen, unheard.

What a wonderful adventure
you have embarked on.
I look forward to meeting you in person
holding your little hand one day
on a Cuban beach
for a heart-to-heart about freedom
and the prices paid.

With love, Grandpa Tai

José Martí

José Julián Martí Pérez, was born in Havana, January 28, 1853 and died in military action in the now famous Dos Rios battle, on May 19, 1895. He is one of Cuba's most famous national heroes and an important figure in Latin American literature. In his short 42 years, he was a poet, an essayist, a journalist, a translator, a professor and a publisher, but most importantly he was a revolutionary activist. Through his writings and political movement, he became a symbol for Cuba's struggle for independence from Spain. To this day he is revered as the "Apostle of Cuban Independence."

José Martí did not support annexation with Spain or the USA. He espoused complete autonomy. He dedicated his life to the promotion of liberty and total political independence for Cuba, and intellectual independence for all Spanish Americans. He died in the fight for his cause. In his death, in the third war of independence, he became the ultimate symbol for the battle for independence. His death stirred the struggling forces to victory, ultimately winning total independence from Spain.

A Pilgrimage to the José Martí Monument

As part of one of my two month stays in Cuba I had the singular desire to make a, bicycle trip, a pilgrimage to Dos Ríos, the place where José Julián Martí Pérez – José Martí – died in battle. I simply wanted to make a respectful trip to visit the place where this great man of historic significance fell in battle with a side bar of sightseeing on the way and maybe add a trip to Santiago de Cuba at the end. In theory the plan was sound and not complicated. Manuel, Eric and I would bicycle, first to Bayamo, the second day to Dos Ríos but stay the night in Palma Soriano, then head to Santiago de Cuba for the third night, returning to Holguín by bus after a few days of visiting friends and sightseeing in Santiago.

Sound simple enough? As soon as we set

our itinerary a nagging sense had me search my memory, looking for an age old saying about, the folly of best laid plans?

To fit Manuel's busy teaching schedule the departure day was set for January 27, about a week after Eric's arrival in Holguín – I had arrived in Cuba in mid-December. The coincidence of arriving at the monument on José Martí's birthday, January 28th, would add an interesting philosophical twist. After a more careful look at a map we decided that the long distance between Bayamo and Dos Ríos, with the foothill mountainous terrain, would be too much for one day if we were also going to enjoy the scenery, spend a reasonable time at the monument and still get us to Palma Soriano for the night. Plans had to be tweaked. The new plan had to include faster public transportation from Bayamo and Dos Ríos. This would give us the freedom to bicycle to Santiago de Cuba from Palma on our third day. Ok, good plan!

The Holguín, Bayamo, Arrival and Departure

The first leg of our trip went without a hitch. Our 5am departure took us into the calm, cool, mist-filled morning of the quiet, lamp-lit streets of Holguín. Street sweepers were already busy swishing the gutters with handmade Cubano brooms. Jacketed Cubans floated in the dim light of incandescent moons, on street corners, waiting for their early morning pickup. We sliced our way through dense fog and out of the city. Drenched in the cool haze that dripped from my helmet we bicycled in the silver veil that hung under a sliver moon.

The trip to Bayamo was flat and straight but nonetheless magical. By mid-morning the road was lumpy in a few places with tar repair ridges; it was like trying to peddle through stripes of stiff cold molasses. Each time you passed over one of the sticky stripes your wheels got more and more covered in the glue that wanted to stick you to the road. This simply slowed us down to appreciate the tall emerald green sugarcane swaying gently in the ghostly mist. The morning fog took a long time to lift but finally when we arrived at Cauto Cristo and her grand grey trellis bridge we were blessed by the stately view of a slow meandering river draped with trees. We stopped and contemplated the stunning visual offering; leaning on the cool steel railing we gazed deeply at her ponderous, timeless path to the ocean hundreds of kilometres away.

An eleven o'clock arrival at our Bayamo *casa* was a welcome reprieve from the 30oc and climbing heat. A shower and snooze in air conditioning refreshed us sufficiently. We headed out by one o'clock looking for lunch. A 78 Cuban pesos (pennies over $3) paid for three medium pizzas, a large bottle of pop and a can of cola in a white table clothed, air conditioned restaurant.

Bayamo is an attractive city with a large well preserved, colourfully painted historic centre with cobblestone-paved roads, blocked from traffic that surrounds a large cathedral. Another Bayamo attraction was the long boulevard that hosted every type of store from banks, restaurants and ice-cream parlours to hardware and department stores. This street is also blocked off from traffic with plenty of shaded benches that border sculptures and vine clung trellises.

In the evening we went out to a seafood restaurant with two fellow travellers from Holland. Our shrimp and fish dinners with sardine rice, plantain and a large salad, came to 190 Cuban pesos (just over 7CUC$ for all five of us). The ice-cream parlour was not open for dessert where Manuel and I had $0.20 ice-creams earlier in the day.

The next day, our second day, was an adventurous day of misdirection. As planned we were up and having breakfast at our Bayamo *casa* at 6:50am – fruit, cheese, bread and coffee milk was 2.50CUC$ each. By 9am we were at the bus terminal via a miss direction to the hustle-bustling train station. Every other time you turn around in Cuba you can imagine travelling back in time 75 or 100 years. The train station where we simply passed through on our bicycles was filled with horse carts of every description. Hand carts were loaded with bails of who knows what, wheelbarrows were stacked with plantain. Men hunched by with stuffed sacks slumped over stooped shoulders. Concrete bunkers with open counter fronts served food of every description. It was a 100 year old version of the modern food court. No McDonald's hamburgers or Kentucky Fried Chicken were served here. Hand written signs showed the prices for pizza, ham sandwiches, peanut butter bars (Cuban protein bars as Manuel calls them), guarapo, pastries and the list goes on.

Smiling and Waving in a José Martí Birthday Parade

Oh guess what, we three managed to march in a José Martí parade. We were on our way to the bus terminal on our bikes. We were standing at an intersection waiting for traffic to move when all of a sudden hundreds and hundreds, a throng one might call it, of Cubans were marching on mass, smiling, cheering waving. For a moment we simply smiled and waved back. Then all of a sudden the group that was passing in front of us were all pushing their bicycles. Hundreds of Cubans pushing their bicycle in the parade, smiling and waving. We had bicycles, we could smile and wave. Without hesitation we deeked into the parade. Alongside the hundreds of others we smiled and waved to the crowds on the sidewalk. It was hilarious fun. When we arrived to our bus terminal destination we simply deeked out of the parade. I managed to park my bicycle and get my video camera out to take some pictures of hundreds of school children, yes smiling and waving as they marched. Here we were on our pilgrimage to the José Martí memorial and we got to march in his birthday parade – how remarkable, how wonderful.

We arrived at the bus terminal just in time for a transport truck that was heading past Dos Ríos, our José Martí memorial destination. The truck was blue with a bright red name tattooed to the back – the Black Dog. Three minutes later and we would have missed the opportunity to be the first to board. Because we were with our bicycles we needed to be first on so that the three bicycles could be stowed at the front of the truck with seated passengers. Two bicycles fit over the space above the cab, with mine standing in the middle isle knee to knee with passengers. The truck fit 60 people sitting on four narrow wooden benches shoulder to shoulder with 15 to 20 standing in the middle aisle with my bicycle. A man with a live turkey pushed his bag under my seat beside the crate of tomatoes and the bundle of plantain. A woman with a three month old baby fumbled her way onto the bench behind me where a 95 year old woman sat with her cane hooked to the hand rail attached to the ceiling. We were not about to depart until every square inch of available space was filled.

Departure from Bayamo at Watermelon Splatting Speeds

Morbid thoughts of Canadian newspaper headlines describing a fatal crash in Cuba with Canadian tourists had to be pushed from thought as we careened down the highway at watermelon splatting speeds. Fumes and dust filled the canvas covered truck that reminded me of a military convoy transporting troops to the front lines. Comfort and safety were not on the list of people-transport concerns when they added benches to this or any other flatbed truck that was designed to carry bananas or sacks of sugar. Finally after two hours and many long moments of prayer we arrived at our destination. Bicycles were liberated over the heads of passengers from their rattled horizontal position. I called out "*Adios, mi amigos*" to the passengers that remained on the truck for the continued trip to Santiago de Cuba. In some ways 120 Cuban pesos ($5) for three men and three bicycles was almost too much to pay though necessity may put me squeezed, shoulder to shoulder, again in the future.

Even though I am writing this in my air-conditioned room at *mi casa*, no one can accuse me of being a totally pampered tourist. A tourist bus might have cost as little as 6 – 8CUC$ each if we could have scheduled one. This ride once again taught me something about the Cuban people and the country and the necessity or maybe the inevitability of hardship and how it changes people and culture. I am reminded of a Canadian woman that was sitting on a subway train annoyed at the person beside her for sitting so close that their hips were touching or the frown of annoyance when a subway traveller accidentally bumped into someone when the train lurched. In conversation with Cubans I have mentioned the concept of "private space" and how it is totally different in North America. It is jealously protected and demanded.

Liberated from the Transport Truck in Dos Ríos

Shade was sparse. People hovered in the 35oc parking lot leaning under the eaves of buildings in the noonday sun. Manuel headed over to the sandwich booth to ask directions for us to bicycle to the José Martí memorial. Manuel's hands were quickly planted at his waist. A few seconds later both hands were raised to the cloudless sky, then his left hand pointed up the road. More gesticulations ended with hands on hips, hat crushed in fist. Manuel walked across the hot dusty parking lot to where we stood with a clenched water bottle in the shade. "We are in the wrong place!" huffed Manuel. "Can you believe it we are in the wrong place? There is another Dos Ríos but it is some 30km back from where we just came. How could this be? Dos Ríos is where he died and this is Dos Ríos, the town of Dos Ríos. The town where two rivers join, Dos Ríos. The history books all say he died at Dos Ríos." Hands flapped to his side in resignation. "I even Googled it. I even checked with geography and history professors."

Dos Ríos is the place but everyone at the lunch counter is chuckling and pointing up the road from where we just came. Manuel, still justifiably sceptical, walks across the road to a truck driver and consults with him. He points up the road from where we had just come.

Specifics are still a bit sketchy but it looks like we have to back track at least 30km, almost half of the distance that we just travelled in that wretched truck. We are not going to get to Dos Ríos today and back to Palma Soriano for the night and still make Santiago de Cuba the next day. Plans have to change. Manuel and I are steadfast in our pilgrimage resolve to see the José Martí monument. Eric seems to be steadfast in his resolve to continue on to Santiago.

Parting Ways

My mother hen instincts start to kick in. Eric, a Canadian, with very limited Spanish should not be on his own. Manuel and I squelch the idea of him bicycling to Santiago on his own – too hot, too far, too many unknowns, just not a good idea. The Palma

Soriano bus terminal is only a 2km bike ride away. Eric decides to go there and find public transit. I hope he finds something more sophisticated than the truck we just got out of. The irony is that the truck we just departed from was going to Santiago de Cuba as its final destination.

Eric's resolve to go it alone cannot be compromised. He is not inclined to come with us and finish the Dos Ríos pilgrimage. I have to give up my mother hen balking and trust that he will be fine on his own. He departs with hesitant good luck pats on the back from Manuel and me. We cross the street and waved to Eric as he disappears to the east. We head in the opposite direction biking to the Cuban transit stop a half km down the road.

Dos Ríos, the other Dos Ríos here we come! Manuel talks to the official transit truck stopper guy who hails down vehicles of every description, matching destinations with passengers and drivers. Thirty minutes later we are hoisting our bikes over the railing of an empty gravel truck. Clenching to the front railing of the truck we head west; the sun and the Sierra Maestra

Mountains on our left. The wind and freedom are exhilarating. Whisked out of ponderance into affirmative action; we are heading to Dos Ríos and nothing is going to stop us from finishing our pilgrimage.

Heading
to the Real
Dos Ríos

The small city of Contramaestre is as far as our grey gravel truck is going but 15km up and down hills in full sun in 35oc heat is to be avoided when possible especially when one has a sun-setting deadline and an unwavering destination. In Contramaestre, after dusting ourselves off, we find a pizza stand with very respectable hot pizza on one side of the street with ice cold guarapo on the other side of the street. What a great lunch, especially for 25 cents. Twenty minutes later we are back on the highway with lifted spirits heading in what we hope is the right way to the other mythical Dos Ríos. A bit out of town Manuel is inclined to go into a school and ask the teacher for confirmation about our destination. Indeed we are on the right track.

Tem kms later after peddling up one long, very long, constant hill we pull over at the town of Baire for further directions. Yes indeed we are going in the right direction but. Yes there was bound to be a BUT – it is further than we expected AND we have to travel over some formidable foothills that will make our last 10km look like knolls in a golf course. We are now standing at 4pm with some 20km of steep bike pushing ahead of us. We are chest pounding men and our egos are big but we want to arrive at the monument in the light. Where will we spend the night let alone will we have enough water.

All along we have been trusting people that don't have cars or maybe no real concept of how far a km really is. I convince Manuel that we should walk up the street and talk to some men mulling around some cars. Maybe they will know where Dos Ríos is and how far we have to go. One would think that the closer we get to the monument the more likely it is that someone would be able to give us accurate directions. One chat followed by hand waving up the road followed by chuckles and smiles led us from one person to another. Eventually someone offered us a 10CUC$ ride to the monument, even with our bikes. Another 5CUC$ will get us from the monument back to the highway but only to the small city of Jiguani in the wrong direction away from Santiago de Cuba. Finishing this trip with going to Santiago de Cuba is starting to look less and less likely. Ok, ok, let's do it. We will figure out the next step later after we see the monument.

Into the Red
Chevrolet We Go

We took the wheels off of our bikes and slipped one frame and four wheels into the trunk and one frame into the back seat with our bags. Manuel and I sat up front with the driver. Before we could hit the highway we had to push start the red beast and head back into town to buy some black market gasoline for the trip. We drove through the middle of a baseball game in progress, through a distant field into a ramshackle backyard where old metal car and truck parts were strewn from pillar to post, hanging on trees and stacked in piles. The driver backed the car into the tight driveway lined with rusty springs so that he could get an easy push start after filling up.

Two little girls hung out among the scrap metal parts. One of them looked me straight in the eye and said "You F... Head." I presumed from the innocence that beamed from her bright eyes that she had no idea what she had just said. It might be the only English that she knows and thought it meant "How are you?" We got back into the car after a push start and headed over the same huge potholes we had earlier straddled, towards the highway. Dos Ríos, the final leg of our journey, here we come.

Thank divine Love for all that is good, that we were led into the lumpy seat of this man's red Chevrolet / *Chevrolet rojo*. After a 20 minute speedy drive west, up and down some major hills, along the main highway, we turned north onto a paved secondary road that was a squeeze, just wide enough to fit two cars. The road was so desolate that we never once had to pull over for a single oncoming car though twice we had to pull off of the road for hay wagons that billowed with the sweet aroma of freshly harvested grass. In an instant we were transported back to the 1600s. Broad brimmed straw hats bowed to us with a generous smile as we waited their gentle passing. Only twice in thirty or forty minutes did another car and then a van, with new suspension, zip past our plodding journey around car-pit-size potholes.

With spine crushing thuds we hit pothole after pothole. One time after my head hit the ceiling of the car I asked Manuel to translate a comment to the driver. With a smile I said that for every crashing pothole thud I would deduct one peso from his driving fee. The driver laughed with us. The very next pothole that he crashed through I yelled "Un peso!" We all laughed. A minute later I yelled "Un peso". Eventually, after yelling "Un peso!" four or five times he got the gist of my meaning and began to slow down as he entered and exited large potholes. His car was 50 or 60 years old. I guess he was not at all afraid that he would break the car in half one of these thuds.

Sometimes the road was so steep that the driver had to put the car into first gear to slowly crawl to the top of what I call a

Cuban mini-mountain only to creep gently down the other side to a fresh valley brimming with green, carved by a sparkling sliver of a river. I can't imagine that we could have possibly made the trip on our bicycles before the end of the day. At long last, after retracing our path after a wrong turn into a turn-of-the-century farm-area, we finally made it to our destination.

Pilgrimage Completed

We pulled into an absolutely humungous parking lot – deserted. Not a single other car was there. Any ceremonies that might have happened on this, José Martí's birthday, were long finished. Not even stragglers remained. Along one edge of the parking lot where the ground swiftly sloped down into the lush valley there were a few students, apparently camping as part of a José Martí event that was designed to teach the students about the rough camping life of an insurgent independence fighter. With a gentle coasting rumble we stopped in front of our pilgrimage destination. Before us stood a pristine, white, monolithic pillar surrounded by a large geometric, walled garden. A black, unlocked metal gate freely swung open as a welcome greeting to this consecrated place. There was a calm sense of sanctification that raised the hairs on the back of my neck as we approached. Was this the result of anticipation, expectations fulfilled? Was this all in my imagination or was this truly a remarkable place? The grounds and even the

garden that surrounded the monument were rather unremarkable, maybe partly because of how straw-dry the grass and shrubs were. I have to admit that I expected a monolithic monument considering the apostle status that Cuba had raised this man to but myth had prepared me for a cairn of stones stacked by thousands of respectful devotees that trod the same pilgrimage journey that we did.

Humming birds buzzed in the bushes that led us silently to the base of the monument, flitting in and out of pink flowers that flourished remarkably well in the parched arid soil. In many ways it was wonderful that we were here alone. Even the driver of our saviour red car stayed behind while we meandered in quiet reverence. We could not have been led here on a better day. The sky was a brilliant Cuban blue with a slight flutter in the flag, puffing to life just at the right moment for me to take a picture with the red, white and blue over the piercing white.

The boyhood still in me can imagine José Martí with fellow insurgents galloping into the arms of fate. Tall grass swaying, shrieks of war trembling through royal palms, a trumpet blasting the advance. Horses whinnying in fear, screams of wounded men and then three fateful bullets taking the life of a great philosophical leader. Blood, heart pounding, then stillness as yet another Cuban soul bled to the sky.

I took a few photographs, a long video of Manuel talking in front of the monument; I wondered and pondered the meaning of life and death and the blood stained earth. Was the ground I walked on worth this man's life? Was it worth any life or the spilling of blood? The pacifist in me can only shrug with unknowing. All I can know is the monument and the journey was every inch worth the detours and false starts it took to arrive. Our pilgrimage was fulfilled and I was left with a sad sense of awe that I will never live down.

Heading to Jiguani

The next leg of our journey was just about as uncertain and backward stepping as the first. We were prodded by our driver of el Chevrolet rojo that we did not have much longer to linger at the monument. He reminded us that he did not have lights in his car. Well that is not quite accurate, he had lights but he did not have a battery in his car and in fact had no belt from his motor to his alternator. No belt and no battery meant that he could not run the lights and dark was descending – time to go. As promised, with the extra 5 CUC$ fee, he would drive us from the monument, about 30 minutes, to the bus terminal in the small town of Jiguani (sounds like Yehwane). From there we would have to figure out the next leg of our trip.

On arriving at the Jiguani bus terminal our first enquiry was about renting a room – there were no rooms for rent. Second enquiry was about buses, back to Bayamo where we started 12 hours ago, back to Holguín where we started two days ago or Palma Soriano or further to Santiago de Cuba. The fast answer for all four destinations was no busses until morning. We did not relish spending a hungry night under a bare fluorescent light at the bus terminal. The next set of queries was Manuel asking about cars that would take us from this place of nowhere to somewhere. Busses, Trucks, Wagons and Cars pulled into the parking lot but no one was going anywhere until finally after shrewd negotiations Manuel secured a ride back to Holguín. We stowed our already disassembled bicycles into the white Lada and headed off to pick up a buddy of the driver that was interested in a free ride to Holguín to visit his sister.

A Weeping Greeting

By now the night was cool, clear and calm. Stars and a drooping moon hung over the purple horizon. There was very little traffic on the road. The hum of tires on pavement was a tranquil melody of contentment that melted in harmony with chirping, cricket filled fields. Before very long Manuel and I were in a head bobbing sleep. On our arrival we were greeted by the shrill cries of Pappy, Pappy, Pappy. Pablo jumped into Manuel's arms to give him a tear-streaked hug.

Holguín, Cuba 2003 Vignette #1

A pretty fourteen-year-old Cuban girl, black hair draped over shoulders, sits on a stoop waiting for a bus to take her home. It will be crowded at this time of day. She chats with an attentive boy from school. He eyes her with the lust of any adolescent boy from anywhere in the world. He tolerates the conversation just to be with her. Her school uniform is tidy but obviously worn; gold skirt, a white shirt that looks like it belongs to her brother. A gold, perfectly pressed scarf tied loosely across shirt does not disguise her growing breasts. She pouts with frustration of waiting in the heat and dismisses the boy's advance of a friendly stroke on shoulder. She is more interested in the puppy that scampers through the puddle in her direction. The boy is annoyed with his diminishing chances of gaining favour with her on this occasion. On impulse he pulls the puppy close realizing the gold mine in his grip. His genius is instantly rewarded as she sprawls on him and coos over the floppy ears. A bus pulls up, destroying any opportunity of exploitation.

Holguín, Cuba 2003 Vignette #2

Splats of oil sizzle violently as a stooped, grey-haired grandmother, a little plump, tosses slivers of plantain into spitting pot. She pulls back quickly as smarts of oil land on her arm. Nudging the plantain with the handle end of a wooden spoon she lets them sing until they are golden brown. One by one she plucks them from the pan onto a waiting plate. The process is repeated until there is enough for the entire family. Some she takes out and mashes into patties with salt, tossed into a black cast iron frypan they are browned for serving. Smashed banana, as they call it, is a staple, for some a delight.

Holguín, Cuba 2003 Vignette #3

Three young men sell meat from their parallel market stoop. They duck with fear from time to time but they have never been stopped. They vigorously wave away a dozen flies that hover. A lady picks up one of the pieces with her finger tips, turns it over for prudent inspection, waving away more flies in the same motion. To their delight she digs in her purse for a five peso note. The twenty cent transaction for dinner has been completed and all are pleased. The small slab of pork that has baked in the sun for hours can almost crawl into a bag on its own volition. Inexpensive at twice the price she will feed four with a prayer. Boiled with rice and onions she will make it palatable. Served with smashed bananas and beans they will all be grateful.

Holguín, Cuba 2003 - Vignette #4

A family of six or eight sit in blank banality mesmerized by the glare of TV. The blue haze of Fidel flickers, burning time stained walls as he gives, what seems to me, the outsider, yet another daily speech. He slams the all-pervasive drug and gun infestation of Miami. He bashes the corruption of the evil U.S. of A. He warns against the self-centered, self-seeking, self-serving temptations of the capitalist regime. His patriots are motionless in their contemplation transfixed by his numbing prosaic platitudes of vapidity. His voice mingles with the chickens clucking in the back yard, fussing with the evening traffic that continues to whir in the front. These are the perpetual songs of Holguín, Cuba that chant the common man to sleep every night and wake him in the morning. When Fidel is finished spouting his requisitions they will all retire for the night. Only half of the family works but they are all drained. The exhaustion of the day takes a toll on everyone, especially the unemployed. Tomorrow the blue flickering haze of Fidel will be the same, the pronouncements will be the same, the substance, the drift, will all be the same. Nothing will change; all will be the same in the morning.

Holguín, Cuba 2003 - Vignette #5

Fifteen people stand in coiled line at the post office waiting for their turn to use ill-afforded email. An expense born on the hopes of contact with seemingly wealthy friends in the off-island world of affluence. For some it is a welcome respite in the air-conditioned, marble-countered room of a modern building but for others their wait is filled with fear of the inevitable e-crash that will lengthen their time wasted in yet another lineup of life. A young boy sprawls on his belly on the cool grey stone floor scratching with a stick in the corner where the floor meets the aged wall. Another boy, maybe brother, sits on his bum bouncing up and down as if on an inanimate chair. The brother does not complain but you can tell he is annoyed. A black-haired man reads the paper, still clutching a bag of oranges, glances at his watch, taps his toe to the tune of impatience. Another man, skinny, eats his greasy cinco-peso pizza clenched by a small piece of scrap paper; this will be his only dinner though he will stand in yet another line for a mango juice on his way home. A plump tired woman slumps on her bench, knees pressed together, feet splayed with a big bag of bread between. There are only three out of five computers working today but this seems to be the norm. The line lengthens as time spills into hours of waiting. It will be after 10pm before there is a quiet lull in the lobby when keyboards stop clicking. Tomorrow the line will start again.

Holguín, Cuba 2003 Vignette #6

A burly man of fifty-five, jet black hair, lays, splayed on his back, face up, on the road, nose pressed to oil pan, feet sticking out from his 1955 Chevrolet. This could have been the car that rolled off the production line in Detroit the day he was born. He tinkers to keep it alive with ill equipped tools and make shift parts that he fashions with his own ingenuity. Purple-black oil runs down his arm, drips from his elbow onto pavement. Dust from ongoing traffic chokes him as he works to keep his life line pumping. No car, no passengers, no taxi fees earned, no chicken for dinner, no milk for his baby. He is a "parallel market driver", always looking over his shoulder. "I can't let you off right out front of your hotel, I will get caught, right here is ok *señor*?"

From Holguín to Gibara
and Back Again

I have travelled back and forth between Holguín and Gibara more times than I can possibly remember by cab, truck and bike. Rock outcroppings, hills and mountains, palm trees, jungle and infinite panoramas still thrill me every time as I weave my way on winding road. The small town of, Floro Perez, is a slower-pace, rural, halfway-point; a town where people live at a meander-pace. A man fixes shoes in the shade of a broad-armed tree. A yellow panted woman carries a large basket of tomatoes on her head across the street to her destination, unknown to me. An old lady waves to her little grandson, *el niño*, to stay on his side of the street, she has buns hammocked in her apron. Maybe his lunch. I love the calmness of my young driver and suggest – *No rapido nesesario señor.* He slows down. He is wearing bright red pants. I wish I dared to be so bold as to wear, *pantalones de color rojo brillante*, but at a stout 60 I am not sure I have the coconuts to pull it off. We just passed a hill that I have biked down many times at wind swept speeds, a blinding curve to the left. I am always exhilarated by the speed, the blind curve in the road and knowing that Gibara is now in sight. I call the next stretch in the highway "Heroes Row" where 15 to 20 cement billboard monuments respectfully commemorate fallen heroes of the revolution – it is moving. Then there is the 100 year old train tunnel built when Gibara was a bustling city. I always take a cool slow ride through the rocks. On the way back with the same driver in red pants we followed a truck full of chairs. It seemed to be why we were going so slowly. Seventy-five chairs travelling in a small truck at a snail's pace but finally the bend in the road revealed that we were travelling behind a red Ford, circa 1953, with a mattress on the roof pulling a small trailer full of household items. I guess it was moving day for someone. In the backseat of my ride home was a mother with a three-year-old, girl, quiet, both with no English. We followed the chairs for fifteen minutes until we passed and instantly got stuck behind a huge transport truck carrying road construction equipment. Then we learned just how slow, slow could be. A spindly winter poinsettia in full bloom creeps over cement wall. A small spotted pig rummages, furrows for morsels, finds hope in hidden scraps. School yard quiet at 5:30pm. Baby and mother still asleep when we arrive at my Holguín destination.

The Round

Dedicated to Stanley Jasspon Kunitz

February 14, 2014

My Dear Lionel:

Happy Valentine's Day.
I am on my way home
from Cuba from my life
swept adventure of swaying
palms, horse carts and fresh
warm fruit. You are less than one
month old, living
your first days. In the spirit
of Stanley Kunitz's poem,
"The Round" he reminds us
with these words to live
each day, every day as a new
day. "I can scarcely wait
till tomorrow / when a new life
begins for me / as it does
each day / as it does
each day." Today all
you can possibly do is live
each day as a new day, as a
new life. Beginnings are truly all
you have, beginnings,
beginnings and more beginnings.

As a new life begins for you,
as it does each day, as it does
each day for me, for
you, for all you can do is live
each day, each day.

Your truly,
Grandpa Tai

Richard M. Grove – known to friends as, Tai, 1953, Hamilton born, lives in Presqu'ile Provincial Park with writer, editor wife, Kim. He is an active photographer/writer/editor/publisher. He has 14 book titles to his name and his images have been used as cover art for almost 75 books. He has had over 100 poems and essays published in periodicals around the world as well as having been published in over 30 anthologies.

He runs his publishing company Hidden Brook Press at <www.HiddenBrookPress.com>. He is the president of the CCLA – Canada Cuba Literary Alliance, a former president of the CPA – Canadian Poetry Association and the founding president of BAC – the Brighton Arts Council. He was a VP of the Toronto Chapter of the CAA – Canadian Authors Association, a board member of IFPOR – the International Festival of Poetry and JMA – Just Muse Arts.

He jokingly boasts that his only claim to fame is that he has been published with Margaret Atwood in "Tough Times", an anthology published by Black Moss Press.

Other Cuba related books by Richard M. Grove

- **View of Contrasts**
  - ISBN - 1-894553-02-0
- **A From Cross Hill**
  - ISBN - 978-1-897475-15-7
- **a trip to banes, cuba**
  - ISBN - 978-1-897475-02-7
- **Trapped In Paradise**
  - ISBN - 978-1-897475-57-7

- **In This We Hear The Light**
  - Cuba photography by Richard M. Grove
  - Cuba poems by John B. Lee
  - ISBN - 978-1-897475-96-6

Other books by Richard M. Grove

- **Beyond Fear and Anger**
  - ISBN - 0-9699598-0-X
- **Poems For Jack**
  - ISBN - 0-9682496-6-3
- **Sky Over Presqu'ile**
  - ISBN - 1-894553-51-9
- **The Family Reunion**
  - ISBN - 978-1-894553-90-2
- **The Importance of Good Roots**
  - ISBN - 978-1-897475-97-3
- **Psycho Babble and the Consternations of Life**
  - ISBN - 978-0-9732522-2-4

- **North of Belleville**
  - Photography by Richard M. Grove
  - Haiku by James Deahl
  - ISBN – 978-1-897475-79-9

www.ingramcontent.com/pod-product-compliance
Lightning Source LLC
Chambersburg PA
CBHW060500080526
44584CB00015B/1494